Acknowledgements

The Mindfulness Initiative is very grateful to the following contributors and reviewers for this report:

Contributors

Kimberley McArthur (Apolitical Foundation), Jutta Tobias (City University of London), Professor Katherine Weare (University of Southampton)

All of the politicians, and the mindfulness teachers from Oxford Mindfulness Foundation and Awaris who have so generously given their time in contributing reflections for this report.

Reviewers

Chris Cullen (Oxford Mindfulness Foundation), Vishvipani Blomfeld (Mindfulness Initiative Wales), Jenny Edwards CBE (Health policy lead, The Mindfulness Initiative), Jim Godfrey (Goddfrey Coaching), Edmund Halliwell (Mindfulness Initiative Trustee), Alan Howarth (Mindfulness APPG Vice-Chair).

Funding

This project was generously supported by the Network for Social Change.

Network for
Social Change
Charitable trust

The work of the Mindfulness Initiative more broadly is supported by the LostandFoundation, Sankalpa and the Mindful Trust.

Copyright © 2023 The Mindfulness Initiative

London, E17, United Kingdom

The Mindfulness Initiative is a Charitable Incorporated Organisation (registered in England and Wales no: 1179834)

Writing: Ruth Ormston & Jamie Bristow
Research: Dr Otto Simonsson
Copy-editing: Ellie Macdonald
Report design: J-P Stanway
Cover credit: yuliagam/shutterstock

This report should be cited as: Ormston, R., Bristow, J. (2023). Mindfulness in Westminster: Reflections from UK Politicians. The Mindfulness Initiative

ISBN 978-1-913353-07-0

 This work is licensed under a Creative Commons Attribution-Non-commercialNoDerivatives 4.0 International License.

About the Mindfulness Initiative

The Mindfulness Initiative provides the secretariat to the Mindfulness All-Party Parliamentary Group. The initiative works with legislators around the world who practice mindfulness and helps them to make trainable capacities of heart and mind serious considerations of public policy. We investigate the benefits, limitations, opportunities and challenges in assessing and implementing mindfulness and compassion training and educate leaders, service-commissioners and the general public based on these findings. Visit www.themindfulnessinitiative.org.uk to find out more.

The Mindfulness Initiative is a charity that receives no public or government funding. If you would like to support our work in putting mindfulness and compassion at the heart of public life, please visit https://www.themindfulnessinitiative.org/Appeal/donate or email us at info@mindfulnessinitiative.org.uk

About the Writing & Research Team

Ruth Ormston
Ruth Ormston is director of The Mindfulness Initiative, and the main liaison for the Mindfulness All-Party Parliamentary Group. Ruth is also a founding member of the UK's Mindfulness in Law Group. Previously a solicitor in a large city law firm, and a mindfulness teacher, Ruth has a particular interest in the impact that mindfulness and compassion can have on the capacities of leaders and decision-makers.

Jamie Bristow
Jamie Bristow served as the Director of the Mindfulness Initiative from 2015 to 2023, staying on as a policy expert on climate and sustainability matters. In 2023, he joined the Inner Development Goals to lead on policy and advocacy. Jamie has authored a series of influential publications on mindfulness and collaborates with decision-makers around the world to integrate inner capacities and contemplative practice into the public realm.

Dr. Otto Simonsson
Otto Simonsson is a postdoctoral researcher at Karolinska Institutet, where he conducts experimental and epidemiological research on meditation. He is broadly interested in the spread of meditation in society and its effects on democracy. More specifically, he investigates the prevalence of meditation use in different countries and the effects of mindfulness-based and kindness-based interventions on affective polarization and other political intergroup biases.

Contents

Foreword 5

Introduction 6

1 Individual Benefits 8
    1.1 Performance 10
    1.2 Resilience 12

2 Relationships with others 16
    2.1 Responding vs Reacting 18
    2.2 Better Listening 20
    2.3 Navigating Disagreement 21
    2.4 Connecting Through Collective Experience 22

3 Parliamentary Culture 26
    3.1 Mindfulness in the Debating Chamber 28
    3.2 Counteracting Tribalism and Polarisation 30
    3.3 Reconnecting to Values, and the Wider World 33

4 Where Next for Mindfulness in Politics? 34

Conclusion 36

Recommendations 37

Appendix 40

References 42

Foreword and Introduction

September 2023

In the years we've served as Co-chairs of the Mindfulness All-Party Parliamentary Group, we have overseen a number of policy inquiries in which leading experts and people with personal experience of evidence-based mindfulness training have attested to its multiple benefits across various domains in public life. After recognising some of these benefits for ourselves, it was perhaps natural for members of the all-party group to start asking what the impact of mindfulness training has been, or could become, within Westminster itself. As such, we are delighted that this report has captured the views of our colleagues on the impact of the mindfulness training that was first introduced in Parliament over 10 years ago.

We are grateful to colleagues who have taken the time to share their reflections: it is moving to read of the practical ways they have deployed mindfulness training and techniques to support them in their roles. Perhaps most profound is how they speak of mindfulness training helping them improve interpersonal relationships and navigate disagreement; as well as its potential impact on wider political culture. In an era of increasing polarisation, these insights serve as a reminder that underneath our differences, many of us yearn for a deeper level of connection - with ourselves, those around us, and with the wider world.

What would the impact on collective decision-making be if, in addition to robust debate, there was also greater capacity in Westminster for listening? How much more effectively might ideas be tested and creative solutions arrived at if we started from a position of 'disagreeing better'? This report explores the potential for mindfulness practices to help answer some of these questions.

We are grateful to the teachers of the mindfulness programme in Westminster for their dedication and support with the mindfulness training programme throughout the years, to Professor Lord Richard Layard and former Member of Parliament Chris Ruane for initiating the programme in the first instance, to the Speakers of both Houses and the Health and Wellbeing Services Team in Parliament for their support, and to the Mindfulness Initiative for pulling together this account of politicians' experiences to date.

As well as acting as a public record, we hope that this report facilitates the further development of mindfulness training in Westminster, so that its benefits can be experienced by generations of politicians to come, and by extension the wider communities they serve.

Jessica Morden MP
Co-chair of the Mindfulness All-Party Parliamentary Group and Labour MP for Newport East

Tim Loughton MP
Co-Chair of the Mindfulness All-Party Parliamentary Group and Conservative MP for Worthing East and Shoreham

Introduction

"We talk about mindfulness being helpful 'out there', but what about how mindfulness could help 'in here', in Parliament? What about mindful politics?"

– Ruth Lister, Baroness Lister of Burtersett

In the UK, public trust in politicians is at a record low, while a majority of citizens report a dislike of "how politics works" acting as a barrier to personal engagement.[1] Add to this media portrayals of toxicity in Westminster, and the resulting picture is at odds with one in which politicians from across divides sit respectfully together, exploring the workings of the mind and heart to cultivate increased presence, awareness and care. But that is what a significant number of politicians have done over the past ten years, by participating in mindfulness training.

To date, mindfulness courses or classes have been attended, voluntarily, by over 300 Members of the House of Commons (MPs) and House of Lords (Peers) from diverse political backgrounds, as well as approximately 800 staff members.

Drawing on reflections given by around 20 politicians during in-depth interviews, as well as comments made elsewhere, this report is the first attempt globally to comprehensively set out accounts from politicians on the personal and interpersonal benefits of their mindfulness training. Many of these align with existing research in psychology, neuroscience, and leadership development.

Chapter One considers the ways in which politicians report that their mindfulness training has positively impacted individual wellbeing and performance, with **Chapter Two** detailing accounts of how it may have changed the quality of their relationships and exchanges with others. In **Chapter Three** we explore how the perceived strengthening of politicians' individual cognitive and emotional resources through mindfulness training could have wider implications for parliamentary culture, and help to defuse polarisation, and in **Chapter Four** we consider where next for mindfulness in Westminster. Further details on mindfulness within a political context, including information on the Mindfulness All-Party Parliamentary Group and the Mindfulness Initiative's Global Political Network, are available in the **Appendix**.

The reflections from MPs and peers in this report make a compelling case for evidence-based psychological training, such as mindfulness, to be offered to legislators not only for their own wellbeing and performance, but also in the interests of a healthier political environment. Given that in a representative democracy millions depend upon the cognitive, emotional, and relational competencies of a small appointed group, we suggest that such training is not simply a 'nice to have'. Supporting our leaders to navigate complex issues and conflicting values by investing in their psychosocial resources is in all of our best interests and a vital consideration for the future.

 What is mindfulness?

Mindfulness is a natural capacity that enables people to pay attention intentionally to present-moment experience, inside themselves and in their environment, with an attitude of openness, allowing, curiosity and care. A simple definition of mindfulness belies its foundational nature and influence not only on **what** people pay attention to, but also the qualities of **how** they pay attention to all they experience. Although this innate capacity has long been prized in spiritual contexts, cultivating it in secular life through evidence-based practice has become increasingly important given the proliferation of technologies that consistently hijack our attention.

> "Mindfulness actually pervades most of what we do and that has made a profound difference to me."
>
> – Angela Harris, Baroness Harris of Richmond

1

Individual Benefits

Individual Benefits

"I'm more relaxed. I'm more able to do a higher volume of work. I'm able to move between things more easily and I'm less reliant on other methods to relax, which might involve doing something that's not productive."

– A former senior government minister

Most of the 17,000 academic articles focussed on mindfulness examine its impact on individual mental wellbeing and performance.[2] Interventions like Mindfulness-Based Cognitive Therapy (MBCT) and Mindfulness-Based Stress Reduction (MBSR) demonstrate efficacy on par with prescription drugs in preventing depression (MBCT) and treating anxiety (MBSR) in rigorous trials.[3] While research on non-clinical interventions is not yet as substantial, mindfulness training has positively affected various measures critical to the workplace, including job satisfaction, occupational stress and burnout, emotional intelligence, and compassion.[4] Lab tests have also demonstrated performance boosts to cognitive functions, such as attention, memory and self-control, and changes to the biomarkers of stress.[5]

The experiences of politicians who have undertaken mindfulness training in Westminster align with these findings, with personal and professional improvements reported following regular practice. Politicians refer to the weekly mindfulness parliamentary 'drop-in' class as "respite", an "oasis in a desert" and to it making them happier or better able to return to parliamentary business "feeling stronger, better energised, and more hopeful".

By exploring the reported benefits of mindfulness in terms of **resilience** and **performance** in this chapter, we seek to uncover the potential for mindfulness to enhance politicians' overall well-being and effectiveness within a high-stress environment.

1.1 Performance

"With mindfulness, you can manage those pointless negative thoughts that get in the way of you doing things properly or in the right sequence".

– Elizabeth Andrews, Baroness Andrews OBE

In the clamour of parliamentary proceedings, paying attention to relevant information is paramount for informed decision-making. At its most basic level, mindfulness can be understood as attention training, and thus it's perhaps unsurprising that politicians report increased focus and efficiency as a result of mindfulness practice. Some speak of an ability to prioritise their 'to-do' list more effectively, along with improved 'task-switching': the capacity to cognitively switch from one task to another. One politician comments:

"I'm better and more robust and able to move between things faster."

Those who speak of being more efficient recognise that better attention regulation positively alters both the quality of tasks as well as their duration, with MP and former Conservative Minister for Sport Tracey Crouch observing that:

"Mindfulness makes me much more focussed on the meeting that I'm in (and) actually makes those meetings far more efficient because instead of me saying 'I'm sorry, I didn't quite understand that point', i.e. I wasn't listening, (instead) I'm fully focussed. And therefore, that meeting can be done and dusted in twenty minutes rather than 30 or 40 minutes."

Others speak of being better able to manage their time, with mindfulness enabling them to more frequently "break free from habitual thought patterns," "step back" and to "do more planning". Several politicians discuss the stress that comes with public speaking and how they use mindfulness techniques to alleviate it. They emphasise the practical benefits of this approach – of consciously taking a "mindful pause" before speaking in the chamber. Tracey Crouch MP refers to taking her shoes off before a speech to mindfully feel the ground beneath her feet and 'help anchor' herself to improve performance.

As well as being a self-regulation technique that supports public speaking, the increased sense of self-awareness that comes with their mindfulness practice allows some politicians to experience a greater sense of fluidity within the context of the speech itself:

> "The breathing out, the feet on the floor, the dropping of the shoulders and knowing that there isn't only one way to get it right".

Clive Lewis MP notes that the quality of acceptance emphasised in mindfulness practice has helped him be more forgiving when a TV interview or other high-profile engagement does not go as well as hoped: "It helps me to draw a line under something and move on to the next thing, with fewer self-critical thoughts sabotaging my future performance."

BOX 1: BACKGROUND

The introduction of mindfulness training in Westminster

Since its inception 10 years ago, over 300 Members of the House of Commons and House of Lords from across the political spectrum and around 800 members of their staff have, voluntarily, participated in some form of mindfulness training in the UK Parliament. Between 2013 and 2020, courses were advertised by emails sent to all Members of the Commons and Lords, usually by Members who had previously participated in the programme. Since 2020 they have been advertised by emails and other internal communications sent to Members of both Houses, either by members who have participated or by the Parliamentary Health and Wellbeing Services team.

Mindfulness training first took place in the UK Parliament in early 2013, following a joint approach by Lord Richard Layard, and Chris Ruane MP to Professor Mark Williams from the Oxford Mindfulness Centre, part of the Department of Psychiatry at the University of Oxford. Following meetings in December 2012, it was agreed an eight-session evening mindfulness course would be offered in Parliament from January to March of that year. Richard Layard and Chris Ruane sent an invitation to all Members of the Commons and Lords, inviting them to consider participating.

After positive feedback from members who took this initial course, as well as inquiries from those who weren't able to attend, Mark Williams and Chris Cullen (Oxford Mindfulness Centre) were asked to provide further mindfulness training to Members of both Houses and parliamentary staff. In order to protect both groups' confidentiality, parliamentarians were clear from the start that the staff programme would be separate from that for members. Speakers of both Houses were informed about the courses. The then Speaker of the House of Commons, John Bercow, met with some of those involved in the mindfulness programme in March 2013 and encouraged its further development. This course was taken by around 90 MPs from both Houses over the next 12-18 months. The courses for both groups proved to be popular - the 20 places on the first course for staff were filled within 10 minutes of it being advertised, with a waiting list of 90 forming within an hour.

Until late 2020, the Oxford Mindfulness Centre offered these courses on a pro-bono basis. A tender and procurement process conducted by the parliamentary Health and Well-being team then led to Awaris, a training organisation that specialises in mindfulness and has experience working in political settings, picking up the teaching of the sessions.

1.2 Resilience

"We need to talk to both Houses of Parliament more effectively about why mindfulness isn't just some rather soppy option. It's a very serious opportunity to take stock and to develop resilience and emotional understanding."

– Elizabeth Andrews, Baroness Andrews

Parliament is a demanding work environment. A study from 2016 found that parliamentarians from the UK House of Commons have higher rates of mental health problems than the wider UK population.[6]

The reasons for this perhaps lie in the extraordinary presssures that accompany a life of public service. 92% of UK MPs work over 50 hours a week, with 41% working more than 70 hours a week.[7] They have large volumes of correspondence from constituents and others requiring replies, exposure to high levels of distress and trauma in weekly constituency surgeries, job insecurity, extended time away from home and family, and exposure to public scrutiny and media criticism in carrying out their role.[8] Long hours, constant pressure, high levels of emotional labour, online harassment, and threats of physical violence can lead to significant chronic stress, adversely affecting essential cognitive functions such as emotion regulation, cognitive-flexibility, and working memory.[9]

Despite this, there has historically been, and still may be, some reluctance amongst politicians to talk openly about either stress at work or mental health, perhaps for fear of the exposure it would bring. This reluctance began to noticeably shift in c. 2014 - 2015 when MPs became more open in the Chamber about their mental health issues. This included some who had done the mindfulness course, and commented on the fact the programme contributed to an ethos in which talking about their struggles felt more possible. Harriet Harmann MP spoke to this recently during a public event at the British Library. She commented on finding her own participation in mindfulness classes in Westminster beneficial before reflecting that now there are MPs: "who will stand up in the House of Commons and talk about their own mental health difficulties, and that is such an incredibly important breakthrough".

Many politicians mentioned signing up for mindfulness training in part to help them cope with the pressures of the job and because of a hope that undertaking the course would positively impact their mental well-being. Some speak openly of a wish to reduce their stress levels. Others, such as Tracey Crouch MP refer to a specific mental health challenge like depression as being the catalyst for undertaking a course. Another politician, also commenting in relation to depression, notes that mindfulness was "particularly helpful in dealing with difficulties".

In some cases, MPs and Peers were also curious to learn about mindfulness to better understand the applications for people struggling with difficulties within wider society. Indeed one politician, John Cruddas MP, admits he came to the personal benefits later:

> "I was really interested in its applied public policy implications. And so I did it as a bit of participant observation. But then I could see the personal benefits."

Politicians describe personal benefit from taking classes, emphasising that the practical exercises taught in the course provide a tool for self-regulation and stress management. As one MP reflects: "Ten minutes of practice and all of a sudden, you're in a much better place". Another politician describes the benefits of it going beyond relaxation. "I don't actually like the word 'relax'. I mean, people use it, but it's not really about that for me - It's about knowing where one is, and dealing with that."

> "In an increasingly frantic and complex world, mindfulness allows me to step into the moment and be present – and the importance of doing that should not be underestimated"
>
> – Doreen Lawrence, Baroness Lawrence of Clarendon OBE

BOX 2: BACKGROUND

Details of the mindfulness course in Westminster

The original course delivered to politicians in Westminster by the Oxford Mindfulness Centre was based on the popular and widely-available book 'Finding Peace in a Frantic World' by Professor Mark Williams and Danny Penman.[1] This was an eight-week programme with short sessions and practices that originated from the evidence-based Mindfulness-Based Cognitive Therapy (MBCT) programme, developed by Professor Mark Williams, John Teasdale and Sindel Zegal in the late 1990s. MBCT has been recommended as an effective treatment in the National Institute for Health and Care Excellence (NICE) guidelines for the prevention of relapse of depression since 2004, and is now recommended more widely in the most recent NICE guidelines on depression.[2]

The course currently delivered by Awaris and entitled "Working Mind" is a six-week programme with 60-minute sessions, with a particular emphasis on bringing mindfulness into the heart of working life, supported by neuroscience and an understanding of workplace realities. Weekly themes include Remaining Focussed, Building Emotional Intelligence, Cultivating a Positive Outlook, and Building Social Intelligence.[3]

During both programmes, participants engage in weekly sessions and are guided through teacher-led formal mindfulness practices, including simple body-based meditations. Participants are also encouraged to practise these with guided audio in their own time between sessions, as well as to try out 'informal' practices such as sensing their body while walking, eating mindfully, attending more mindfully to others and to their own experience while speaking and listening, and building resilience by appreciating pleasant experiences. Participants learn about the neuroscience of mindfulness and the ways in which the traits being cultivated during the sessions can be accessed and deployed in everyday living and work life. The sessions are taught in a group setting and led by highly experienced and trained teachers who, in addition to guiding exercises, facilitate dialogue to draw out any emergent learning.

Before the Covid-19 pandemic, mindfulness courses and classes were held in person within Parliament. In response to the pandemic, they moved to an online format. Currently, Members of the House of Commons and the House of Lords can attend two six-week courses annually, while parliamentary staff can attend six six-week courses per year (three for House Staff and three for Members' staff). Awaris offers six-week courses and weekly 'drop-in' mindfulness practice sessions for Members of both Houses. These sessions are available before 9:30am or after 5pm and are open to all Members, even if they haven't taken the six-week course. Similar sessions are held for parliamentary staff.

---

1. Williams, M., Penman, D., Mindfulness: A Practical Guide to Finding Peace in a Frantic World (2011)
2. Depression in adults: treatment and management NICE guideline [NG222] Published 29 June 2022 https://www.nice.org.uk/guidance/ng222
3. https://awaris.co.uk/programmes/employees/workingmind/

"I can breathe in the middle of a sentence. I can actually stop."

– Doreen Massey, Baroness Massey of Darwen

2

Relationships with others

Relationships with Others

"Personally, I find mindfulness very helpful, both in terms of dealing with difficult interpersonal relationships and also just relaxing at the end of the day, even when you've got issues that you're worried about."

– Kate Parminter, Baroness Parminter

Improved relationships are a common benefit that participants report after taking a mindfulness course.[10] Qualitative studies include reports of greater emotional closeness with friends and family, better communication, relating more constructively, reduced anger and increased empathy.[11] The impact of mindfulness training on interpersonal relating, leadership skills, forgiveness, discrimination, retaliation, and conflict resolution has also been documented.[12]

Politicians describe a positive impact of their training on interpersonal relationships both within and outside of Westminster. They report communicating more effectively with constituents, colleagues, and family, demonstrating attentive listening and a higher level of empathy towards mental health concerns. Notably, mindfulness seems to help politicians transcend their immediate emotions and consider the broader consequences of their words and behaviour. Practising mindfulness and sharing their experiences within a group also appears to have fostered an environment in which politicians viewed each other more often as 'human beings', regardless of political affiliation.

In this chapter, we explore the role of mindfulness in providing space to think before reacting, promoting better listening and navigating disagreement in Westminster and elsewhere. We finish with views on how group practice settings particularly facilitate a connection to shared humanity.

2.1 Responding vs Reacting

"It's a blessed gift to be able to create that half-a-second difference between an immediate reaction and a response."

– Chris Ruane, Member of the British Parliament for 20 years and founder of the UK All-Party Parliamentary Group on Mindfulness

In the political arena, quick-wittedness and the ability to think on your feet are often seen as key attributes to success.[13] However, this ability needs to sit alongside the capacity to make sound, robust decisions on issues that impact millions of lives. A tension therefore exists between politicians needing space to consider nuance and complexity, and the expectation that they will provide immediate reactions to criticism and oppositional views in both the debating chamber and on broadcast and social media.

However fleeting or unnoticeable to the untrained eye it would be for a politician to pause before they jump in to speak, many politicians we interviewed speak of the way in which mindfulness training helps them to take a more considered position in challenging situations, rather than just reacting in a habitual, impulsive or knee-jerk manner. In line with academic evidence and personal reports from other workplace contexts, mindfulness training appears to support politicians with responding creatively to situations rather than reacting impulsively.[14] This aligns with established research that shows mindfulness training helps reduce reactive behaviour and enhances creative responses.[15] Indeed, this is perhaps not surprising given that a reduction in reactivity is one of the intended outcomes of the Mindfulness-Based Cognitive Therapy programme, on which the original mindfulness courses in Parliament were based.[16]

One politician refers to their history of "flying off the handle" quite quickly, and notes that mindfulness now "has a really important part to play in my equilibrium… I don't do that so much. I bring it down, and I do it deliberately." They also reflect on the benefits of mindfulness in enabling them to see more clearly the consequences of taking an entrenched and reactive position, beyond their own immediate feelings:

"(more often) I now think: no, no, no, you don't need to do that, you don't need to say that… that will be hurtful… that wouldn't help the situation."

BOX 3: EXPLORE FURTHER

Neurophysiology and the Threat Response

"Fight, flight, or freeze" are psychological terms for the involuntary survival strategies developed in organisms with central nervous systems in reaction to stress triggers.[17] Whilst these nervous system responses to perceived threat or danger may have evolved to ensure survival, they are maladapted to coping with the everyday stresses that exist in modern life. The heightened physiological state that would, historically, have been triggered in response to a physical threat is a much wider risk to overall health if it is engaged much more frequently, particularly in response to anticipated or imagined threats. In these circumstances, the body has insufficient time to return to a safer 'rest and digest' state, where the parasympathetic nervous system is engaged, and the body is soothed to recover.[18] The impacts of this threat response extend beyond the individual, affecting those around them as well. Disordered thinking and perceptual narrowing, which are linked to elevated stress hormones, breathing, and heart rate, contribute to these effects.[19] People in fight-flight mode are more likely to "react," showing less empathy and being less open to other people's perspectives. When individuals are constantly in fight-flight mode, they are also more likely to become prone to extremist views and othering behaviours over time.[20]

MRI scans have demonstrated that mindfulness practice can actively reduce activity in the areas of the brain related to threat response and reactivate the nervous system functions that relax the body after a period of stress and danger, where it might otherwise remain 're-living' or even anticipating ('pre-living') stressful situations.[21]

Feedback from politicians who have undertaken mindfulness training suggests that being able to reduce the habitual impulsive tendencies to 'fight' or 'freeze' enhances their steadiness in the face of political challenges and helps them to navigate disagreement in a manner is perhaps more conducive to active listening and keeping an open mind on issues of complexity.

"I'm much more able to step back and see the other point of view"

– Anna Healy, Baroness Healy of Primrose Hill

2.2 Better Listening

"I think mindfulness has helped me become much better at listening, think about what's going on with the particular person or this particular group, and try to let them talk more about how, for example, a problem might be solved."

– Doreen Massey, Baroness Massey of Darwen

Parliamentarians speak of the benefit that mindfulness has had on relationships both inside Westminster and further afield, including with friends and family.

Mindfulness seems in some cases to help politicians communicate better with their constituents, as they are more able to listen attentively and express empathy towards mental health issues when constituents raise them. They have particularly reported this effect in relation to constituency surgeries, which many MPs often describe as the most challenging time in their week.[22] As Scott Mann MP states:

"I'd like to think that after a stressful week in Parliament, when I'm back on a Friday and I'm doing surgeries and meeting businesses and constituents that I'm a little bit more centred and able to take on board their concerns and deal with them."

Politicians report that their family members noticed a positive change in them after their mindfulness training, and that it helped them handle specific challenges in their family relationships better. One Member of Parliament, for example, speaks of the mental ill-health of a close family member, and the positive impact that their own mindfulness practice has had on their approach towards it, noting: "I was finding situations that were so irrational and so out of my usual understanding... mindfulness gave me the space to stop and think." One politician reflects that if mindfulness could be used to interact better with political opponents, it could surely be used to interact better with friends and family as well whilst another simply concludes that mindfulness made them "more tolerable to live with."

2.3 Navigating Disagreement

"Disagreement is essential and benign and should not be experienced as threatening. It's what debate is about. While MPs know this, of course, many have always appreciated certain havens - APPGs, Select Committees, delegations - in which they can put adversarialism aside and get to know members of the other tribe as real people. Shared mindfulness practice is another iteration of that, but with a distinctive and especially valuable quality because in the nature of this practice we seek together to understand our essential humanity."

– Alan Howarth, Lord Howarth of Newport CBE

The reduction in problematic reactive behaviour reported by politicians after they have undertaken mindfulness training may be in part the result of increased ability to steady themselves, self-regulate their autonomic nervous system and manage their stress before entering challenging conversations. However, other outcomes of mindfulness training also seem to impact the way in which politicians navigate disagreement. For instance, politicians' reports of 'responding' rather than 'reacting' are often accompanied by the sense that they were also "stepping back" and asking questions about the wider picture. As Baroness Parminter puts it: "Mindfulness gives [me] the time to literally calm my body down, to find space, to think: Okay, I'm not going to react immediately… what is that person saying to me and why are they saying it?"

She goes on to say that mindfulness helps her to better understand differences of opinion from the other person's perspective "to see where they're coming from so that you can try and find some common ground". Tim Loughton MP simply reflects that mindfulness helps politicians to "disagree better", and become "better working colleagues in a highly divisive and stressful environment".

2.4 Connecting Through Collective Experience

"I feel quite bonded with the people I did the course (with), which I wasn't expecting. I would talk to them about mindfulness, my mental health and my feelings in a way that I wouldn't have otherwise done. It was quite odd, given (how short the sessions were)."

– A former senior government minister

Politicians report the way in which participating in mindfulness training enables them to see each other as "real people", and subsequently provides a less reactive backdrop for exchanges of opposing views. It seems that mindfulness practices in and of themselves cannot receive all the credit for this. When asked about the training, almost all politicians ascribe at least some of the benefits to both the skill of the teacher holding the space and the group setting itself.

Politicians refer to the psychological safety and support that learning within a group gave them, as well as the support that doing a course within a group setting gave them in between sessions: "I wouldn't have got the same benefits had I not been supported by the group outside the sessions." In some cases, the group provided the incentive to continue the mindfulness training: "it's the group setting, because I wouldn't have bothered otherwise.".

Many politicians identify something unique about the space provided by the mindfulness course that allows them to be themselves, connect with others at the level of their shared humanity and listen more empathetically.

One politician comments that "one of the benefits of it is that it has brought everybody together, and somebody's party politics is completely and utterly irrelevant when you're sitting in the same room with an instructor doing the course...". One instructor simply states that:

"There are not that many spaces, I think, where (politicians) can actually be human beings and be vulnerable and share their own challenges with others in that way."

The group setting appears to have created an atmosphere of psychological safety and trust, in turn enabling some politicians to challenge their long-held attitudes and beliefs towards their colleagues. This was particularly in relation to attitudes held towards individuals from different parties or others viewed as foes. One parliamentarian who undertook mindfulness training admitted being "instinctively anti-Tory" but described a realisation that "underneath all that nonsense going on, they are real people. You have the same pain, the same anxieties, the same worries, the same everything that we all have."

These accounts chime with recent studies suggesting that practising mindfulness can indeed reduce "affective polarisation," which refers to the negative emotions and hostility held towards individuals with opposing beliefs. See Box 6 for more information.

> "It's quite strange to meet your opponents in a more benign climate, which has a different sort of character that is not about having a go at each other. Instead, it's about a common commitment to practices that actually act against the gearing of modern politics."
>
> – Jon Cruddas MP

BOX 4: EXPLORE FURTHER

The neuroscience of mindfulness training

The structure and function of the brain and nervous system are not fixed in childhood: these systems remain 'neuroplastic' i.e. changeable, throughout our lives.[23] These systems can, to some extent, be 're-wired' by our behaviours, habits and experiences, including mindfulness meditation, to improve our cognitive and emotional processes and achieve greater levels of well-being, connection with others, health, happiness and personal effectiveness.

An increasing number of studies, including brain imaging/magnetic resonance imaging (MRI) studies, have explored the impact of mindfulness meditation on brain structures and functions. They indicate that mindfulness meditation can, to an extent, 'rewire' the brain to make neural pathways underlying some key abilities and mechanisms more efficient. The cumulative evidence suggests that meditation can:[24]

1. increase the density, activity and complexity of connections in areas associated with beneficial outcomes such as improvements in attention, self-awareness, self-control, complex thinking, emotional regulation, pain tolerance, introspection, kindness, and compassion.

2. decrease activity and growth in those areas involved in anxiety, hostility, hyper-vigilance, impulsivity and the stress response.

Of particular relevance for the business of politics is the finding that experienced mindfulness practitioners appear to demonstrate both functional and structural differences in emotion regulation networks, correlating with behavioural differences.[25] One particular structure in this network, the hippocampus, is particularly vulnerable to being damaged by chronic stress, creating a harmful feedback loop as negative emotions become more difficult to manage over time.[26] Mindfulness practice appears to bolster the hippocampus, providing an example of improved 'cognitive resilience' that also includes protective benefits to working memory, an important capacity for complex cognitive tasks.[27] Mindfulness meditation has been shown to support other aspects of cognition that are important for decision-making, such as more activity and grey matter in regions associated with learning from past experience.[28] Scientists suggest that these regions may be particularly important in uncertain and fast-changing conditions.

Detailed findings include:

1 Mindfulness meditators have shown more activity and grey matter in the anterior cingulate cortex (ACC) and mid-cingulate cortex, cortical regions involved in attention regulation, emotion regulation, pain control, and self-control.[29]

2 Meditation impacts the rostrolateral prefrontal cortex: a region associated with meta-awareness (awareness of thinking), introspection, and processing of complex, abstract information.[30]

3 Experienced meditators show a greater cortical thickness[31] and greater grey matter concentration in the right anterior insula.[32] This is part of the region responsible for the processing of tactile information such as touch, pain, conscious proprioception (awareness of the position and movement of the body) and awareness of body sensations. This suggests that the ability to pay attention to sensory experience improves.

4 Mindfulness seems to impact the default mode networks, including the ACC, the ventromedial prefrontal cortex and posterior cingulate cortex, a region associated with both emotion regulation and also meta-awareness (the ability to observe thoughts, feelings, sensations and impulses), introspection, and self-referential processing (reflections on your own identity).[33]

5 Mindfulness meditation impacts the amygdalae - two almond-shaped brain structures (one in each hemisphere) associated with the processing of emotional stimuli and linking them to learning and memory. The right amygdala (which particularly responds immediately to perceived threats, sometimes creating an irrational and intense 'emotional hijack' of the brain) is less active and has less grey matter density in regular mediators.[34]

3 Parliamentary Culture

Parliamentary Culture

"Our traditional postures and ways of doing things at Westminster are inimical to the ethos and the wisdom of mindfulness. Reflex adversarialism, tribalism, the whips' regimentation... all these things are working against the grain of what we want."

– Alan Howarth, Lord Howarth of Newport CBE

Researchers have explored the benefits of mindfulness to workplace culture at a number of levels. At the macro level, 'organisational mindfulness' has been studied for over 30 years in contexts where the 'cognitive architecture' of an entire institution is shaped by leaders in a 'top-down' manner; in order to prioritise awareness of, and responsiveness to, potential threats to resilience and reliability.[35] Perhaps more relevant to the parliamentary context however is the 'bottom-up' process of 'mindful organising'; an emergent interpersonal quality that helps loose groups or teams detect and adapt to unexpected challenges and work together while remaining heedful of each other.[36] It is marked by three properties of interrelating: balancing attention to self and others, suppressing personal ego, and a felt quality of attentiveness and continuous learning.[37]

The popularity of mindfulness training in Westminster has led some MPs and Peers to reflect on its influence at collective levels. Accounts suggest it has, at least in some cases, enhanced relevant personal qualities such as empathy, openness to alternative viewpoints, and the seeking of common ground. This seemingly has led to perceived behaviour change beyond the training group environment, manifesting in the debating chamber and in interactions with colleagues from different parties. For some it has challenged the notion of such colleagues as "enemies" and they describe a kinder type of politics, based on respect and thoughtfulness.

The previous chapter summarised the effects of mindfulness on interpersonal relationships related by parliamentarians, reducing conflicts and promoting collaboration. This next chapter explores the observations from politicians on how mindfulness training could influence wider parliamentary culture.

3.1 Mindfulness in the Debating Chamber

"When you're in the House of Commons, and you're debating, and there's someone from the mindfulness class, there's a greater level of respect… the level of the debate actually improves. It is noticeable among people who have done the course".

– Tim loughton MP

Media portrayals of politicians' vitriolic exchanges within the debating chamber make any reports of better listening, presence, attention and care seem implausible. However, for some Members of the House of Commons and House of Lords, participating in mindfulness training changes the perceived tone and quality of debate. One politician notes that: "I will call people out when I feel they need to be called out, but I won't do it on a gratuitous basis as I might have done before…" suggesting that their mindfulness training has led to a different and more positive motivation for expressing disagreement; less related to point-scoring and more to the issues at hand.

Another speaks of mindfulness being: "so powerful in reminding me that I'm dealing with another human being. It helps to remove the mental and psychological barriers that we place when we construct our enemies… They're not our enemies… It's just that, at that moment, we are in different positions, and those positions will change because that is the only thing that is certain: change."

It is clear that parliamentarians have varying perspectives on the cultural and collective benefits that come with mindfulness practice, and, if reported by them, the characterisation of these benefits. Various views are presented on this spectrum, from the belief that mindfulness lends a more courteous tone to political discourse, to bolder statements suggesting a more radical transformation. In an interview for a BBC Radio 4 segment focused on the parliamentary mindfulness programme, former Conservative Minister the Rt Hon Sir Desmond Swayne MP said, "During this Brexit debate, we have been subjected to greater stress, and therefore having a routine that reduces your stress levels is very helpful. It doesn't make me any less ideological. I still have profound differences and disagreements with colleagues… but [mindfulness] does make it possible to function and be civil."

If mindfulness practice becomes simply about being civil to one another, though, some may view this as too limited. Caroline Lucas MP states that if "mindfulness is simply about civility, it's not for me", implying that for her to consider mindfulness worth the investment, it must facilitate a deeper shift in values.

Chris Ruane, who served in Parliament for two decades, also sees potential for cultural shifts. Drawing from his personal evolution over the years, he reports, "many colleagues, including the Speaker of the House of Commons, have remarked on the significant transformation I have undergone over time, likely enhancing the constructiveness of my contributions to debates and increasing the effectiveness and collegiality of my behind-the-scenes work. If mindfulness practice were more commonplace, we'd start to see shifts in how the House conducts itself."

"(Mindfulness) is a technique that raises awareness of one's thoughts and their effects on behaviour towards oneself and others. Perhaps we might want to think about it in this House?"

– Annabel Goldie, Baroness Goldie, speaking in the House of Lords

3.2 Counteracting Tribalism and Polarisation

"It feels to me like (mindfulness) is more important than ever when you've got a politics, certainly in this country, which is becoming ever more polarised. The more that we've got a little bit of a gap between people's identities, if you like, and beliefs they happen to have or thoughts they happen to think, then it feels like there might be a potential at least for politics based on greater respect and thoughtfulness."

– Caroline Lucas MP

Divisive issues like Brexit have created deep levels of affective polarisation in the UK, even where individuals may otherwise agree on salient issues.[38] Accordingly, almost all the politicians we spoke to referred to increasing levels of rigid tribalism and polarisation within political life: "it kind of feels like to be effective, you have to be quite aggressive."

There is increasing evidence that this aggression could be damaging for diversity, with Parliament being viewed even by those who sit within it as less inclusive and supportive for women and those from minority ethnic backgrounds.[39] Nicola Sturgeon and Jacinda Ardern referred to the relentless and brutal nature of politics in their leadership resignation speeches: the fact that they both issued reminders that politicians are 'human beings' within that context was notable.[40]

Politicians report, however, noticing a change in their attitudes and behaviour towards those within their immediate mindfulness training group, partly from recognising their commonality and humanity. This perceived change in attitude toward colleagues from the course even appears, in some instances, to have extended to interactions with each other in the chamber and to interactions with colleagues from elsewhere in Westminster. As one member of the House of Lords put it, "Mindfulness has allowed people in Parliament to work with greater compassion, understanding and patience… and I've noticed that even those who haven't been on the course sometimes adapt to that new tone when joining conversations between those who have."

Some politicians report an improvement in their ability to distinguish their own thoughts from their identity and to apply this approach to the thoughts and opinions of individuals beyond their training group: Caroline Lucas MP, states "I think mindfulness helps you recognise that you are not the same as your thoughts. As such, there's a potential there, at least, to have more useful conversations and to limit the knee-jerk reactions that happen in social media."

BOX 5: EXPLORE FURTHER

'Thoughts not facts'

A well-known phrase used in the evidence based Mindfulness-Based Cognitive Therapy Course widely available across the UK's National Health Service (on which the original parliamentary programme was directly based) is "thoughts are not facts".

This insight arises from the process of 'decentering', or developing metacognitive awareness, which is a well-known element of Cognitive Behavioural Therapy theory and practice. It explicitly encourages individuals to change the nature of their relationship with their thoughts by interrogating their content rather than simply accepting them as being true. Mindfulness-Based Cognitive Therapy made this change in the relationship with one's thoughts even more explicit, by encouraging participants to view thoughts as mental events rather than over-identifying with their content.

The phrase "thoughts are not facts" is not used to suggest that all thoughts are unreliable or to be taken lightly, but suggests that we don't have to automatically believe every thought as an absolute truth. As well as helping to reduce "self-directed, negative propaganda",[41] decentring from thoughts in this way can allow individuals to label a thought as exactly that - something that can be examined 'on the workbench of the mind'. This perhaps enables a wider level of choice over whether and how to respond to a particular thought, rather than simply reacting to it impulsively.

BOX 6: EXPLORE FURTHER

What do we mean by polarisation?

The polarisation or 'othering' of opponents that takes place in Westminster can act as a driver of polarisation and fragmentation in wider society.[42] Similarly, political polarisation can affect social relationships and interaction, increase intolerance, and damage the social fabric of a society and the functioning of democracy.[43] Intractable political conflict can lead to a failure to cooperate on complex, urgent issues that demand a collective approach.[44]

There is a distinction between issue-based and affective polarisation.[45] This is an important distinction to make, particularly in the UK, where the media and individuals use the terms 'polarisation' and 'division' interchangeably and in a generalised way.

Issue-based polarisation describes divisions which form around a particular policy position or issue. The salience of an issue is important, because where it carries more weight relative to other topics (i.e. because a higher proportion of the public care strongly about it) this can impact how polarised a political environment feels.

Affective polarisation, on the other hand, occurs when individuals start to separate themselves socially and distrust or dislike people from the opposing side, regardless of whether or not they disagree on matters of policy. This leads to the creation of 'in-groups' who share a particular opinion with an individual and 'out-groups' who do not.

Two of the key concepts involved in affective polarisation are:

- **identification**, where a person links together a person's attitudes with their identities, associating positive traits with their own 'group' and negative traits with the 'other' group. This process of categorisation aids in the definition of one's own identity, providing a sense of belonging, self-esteem, and a blueprint for behaviour that aligns with group norms.

- **perception bias**, which shapes how people interpret and remember information, influenced by preconceptions, attitudes, and group affiliations. These biases impact individuals' understanding and experience of the world, often leading to differing interpretations of the same event based on their 'in-group' perspective.

Studies have shown that mindfulness training and a befriending meditation which is used in some compassion and mindfulness training has been found to reduce affective polarisation over time.[46] These are small-scale, early studies and more research is needed. However, if their findings are substantiated by further research, the potential implications could be profound.

3.3 Reconnecting to Values, and the Wider World

> "Mindfulness encourages you to take a moment to reflect and think about others… not just in terms of other beings, but in terms of the Earth which we are part of… I'm not claiming that mindfulness will turn you into the next Greta Thunberg, but it might create the space in you to think a little more openly about how you interact with other people and other things…"

– Kate Parminter, Baroness Parminter

Related to politicians' reflections on the relevance of mindfulness to political culture, are their insights on how mindfulness training can help them reconnect to their core values, the fundamental reasons they embarked on a career in politics, or their ambition to be of service to the wider world. Past reports from politicians have included mention of keeping perspective and staying in touch with what is most important to them.[47] One politician reflects:

> "Mindfulness is helpful in terms of its ability to help you stop and take a moment to think about how you react to things and remember that you're there for other people, not for yourself – which is the golden rule, isn't it?"

Another comments that "Mindfulness stops you wanting to own everything and it allows you to be part of change that will go beyond you…"

These reflections chime with an emerging trend amongst mindfulness teachers to broaden the scope of courses to more explicitly include reflection into one's values and interdependent relationship with social context. Sometimes described as 'social mindfulness', the greater awareness developed through practice is directed towards group culture and processes, in addition to the traditional focus on one's own psychology and behaviour. This more contextual framing may be more influential in impacting organisational culture and creating lasting behavioural change than when these themes remain implicit.[48]

4
Where Next for Mindfulness in Politics?

Where Next for Mindfulness in Politics?

"Some unexpected people have become the strongest advocates of the mindfulness course. Even those you may have expected to be cynical and sceptical initially are now its biggest supporters. For something that may be portrayed as alternative, mindfulness is actually very inclusive in terms of bringing people in. There aren't many other groups like that where people look way beyond the politics of it all - it's quite a unifying force."

– Tim Loughton MP

The individuals mentioned in this report are politicians who chose to participate in mindfulness training, found it beneficial, and now incorporate mindfulness practices into their daily lives. While some have made it a daily habit, others only use it during certain times. Many in this group express a desire to practise mindfulness more often than they currently do.

If mindfulness training has the potential benefits reported by the politicians referenced in this report, why isn't everyone doing it, and why aren't those who have been introduced to the practice doing it more often?

When asked why more of their colleagues hadn't undertaken mindfulness training, politicians refer to a variety of factors, including time pressures, a lack of prioritisation for self-care, and a misunderstanding of what mindfulness training is. They felt some colleagues might still consider mindfulness as too alternative - "airy-fairy" and "hocus pocus" are among the words used by politicians in describing this potential scepticism.

Others state that whilst mindfulness might now be widely viewed as "valuable" some colleagues may simply think they do not need it. There is acknowledgement of the fact that mindfulness isn't necessarily for everyone, and people may have their own way of cultivating their inner resources for carrying out their roles.

Some speak positively about the success of the programme in Parliament in a relatively short space of time, and about the number of colleagues who had attended classes or courses: "it really is quite a success story... in terms of the operation of the British Parliament over the years."

Conclusion

"Is mindfulness something that can make a kinder and more effective politics? I would say the answer is inevitably yes."

– Angela Harris, Baroness Harris of Richmond

This report began with the words of Baroness Lister, inviting consideration of how cultivating mindfulness might inform Westminster politics. Or, in other words, how would politicians doing politics more 'mindfully' be any different from business as usual? The accounts of politicians summarised here represent an important first step towards answering this question.

At an individual and interpersonal level, politicians' reports of the impact that mindfulness training has had are compelling. It appears to have boosted performance and strengthened resilience, resulting in politicians feeling better able to face the everyday challenges of their role. Within a context where "more [politicians] struggle than not" due to "job stressors [that] are numerous and severe",[49] they have reported that mindfulness helps them with managing their schedules, self-regulating their stress, calming their nerves before speaking in the Chamber and, after practising together, re-entering the frenetic pace of Parliament feeling "stronger, better energised, and more hopeful". In addition, politicians note that mindfulness provides them with the cognitive and emotional resources to listen to others more effectively and respond creatively rather than react impulsively to more challenging interactions.

The media and the public often show little sympathy for those who choose a life of political service. However, we propose that it's in all of our best interests when those whose decisions impact everyone have robust levels of wellbeing, self-regulation and effectiveness, and that evidence-based psycho-social support, like mindfulness training, should be encouraged.

Beyond this, some politicians have suggested that the relational benefits of mindfulness practice have extended far beyond their immediate practice group. This suggestion that personal mindfulness practice could have a positive impact on wider political culture is hard to demonstrate and remains controversial. What a 'positive impact' looks like is also not something that politicians would necessarily agree on. Nevertheless, the way in which politicians speak of mindfulness helping them to "disagree better", and remember that a person holding opposing views is still a human being, will be welcomed by many. In a recent poll, the public identified 'integrity' and 'listening to diverse views' amongst the qualities they would most like to see more of in politicians.[50] Providing opportunities to develop such qualities through training like mindfulness could, we suggest, contribute to the restoration of trust in how politics functions. As former MP and Government minister, now a Labour peer, Lord Alan Howarth so eloquently identifies:

> "The mutual respect, the willingness to listen, the kindness, the open-minded seeking after better understanding that mindfulness helps inculcate – these are the crucial underpinnings for a better politics."

Recommendations

We recommend that:

1. Good-quality and accessible mindfulness training is offered to policy and decision-makers at all levels of government.

2. Funding should be made available to provide specific mindfulness-based programmes and workshops (such as interpersonal mindfulness) to those politicians who wish to progress their training from the introductory course.

3. Resources should be provided to support politicians with either beginning or maintaining their mindfulness practice, including consideration of a specific physical space for politicians to practice, induction training for new politicians and practice sessions of varying length and frequency, both online and in-person.

4. More research should be conducted on mindfulness in a political context, with particular emphasis on the impact of personal and group practices on organisational approaches and ways of working together.

Appendix

Supplementary information on mindfulness in politics

The Formation of a UK Mindfulness All-Party Parliamentary Group

In 2014, a group of politicians from different political parties formed the Mindfulness All-Party Parliamentary Group (MAPPG) after experiencing the benefits of mindfulness practice during early courses in Parliament. This group convenes to discuss the potential benefits of mindfulness in society and its impact on various policies. The group published a report in 2015, Mindful Nation UK,[51] which explored the evidence supporting mindfulness in areas such as health, education, criminal justice and the workplace. The report also gave policy recommendations relating to these areas. The Mindfulness Initiative policy institute acts as the clerk for the MAPPG - both are separate from the teaching program.

Mindfulness in International Legislatures and Settings

The Mindfulness Initiative has supported politicians and advocates for mindfulness within international legislatures through its Global Political Network,[52] led by former Member of Parliament Chris Ruane, who played a pivotal role in the introduction of mindfulness within the UK Parliament and brings his experience of both that and the MAPPG to the network. This network meets online 2-3 times a year to bring together representatives from different countries who are interested in mindfulness and politics. They share the latest research and evidence on mindfulness, and discuss the best ways to introduce mindfulness in political and policy settings.

The popularity of mindfulness in Westminster, the media attention it has drawn, and the establishment of the MAPPG seem to have inspired politicians in several other legislatures to become interested in mindfulness training. Mindfulness programmes have been introduced in several parliaments, including those of Canada, Denmark, Estonia, Ireland, the Netherlands, and Europe. One notable example is the French National Assembly, where around 100 people have participated in mindfulness training.

In 2017, the Mindfulness Initiative assisted the MAPPG Group in hosting a gathering of politicians from different countries to practise mindfulness and inquire into its implications for public policy and the political process itself. This gathering was attended by 40 politicians from 14 countries and was addressed by Professor Jon Kabat-Zinn, one of the international pioneers of contemporary mindfulness programmes.

References

References

1. Renwick, A., Lauderdale, B., Russell, M. and Cleaver, J. (2023). Public Preferences for Integrity and Accountability in Politics Results of a Second Survey of the UK Population Third Report of the Democracy in the UK after Brexit Project. [online] Retrieved from at: https://www.ucl.ac.uk/constitution-unit/sites/constitution_unit/files/ucl_cu_report3_digital_final.pdf.

2. Baminiwatta, A., & Solangaarachchi, I. (2021). Trends and Developments in Mindfulness Research over 55 Years: A Bibliometric Analysis of Publications Indexed in Web of Science. Mindfulness, 12(9), 2099–2116.

3. Kuyken W, Hayes R, Barrett B, Byng R, Dalgleish T, Kessler D, et al. Effectiveness and cost-effectiveness of mindfulness-based cognitive therapy compared with maintenance antidepressant treatment in the prevention of depressive relapse or recurrence (PREVENT): A randomised controlled trial. Lancet 2015; 386.63–73.

   Hoge, E. A., Bui, E., Mete, M., Dutton, M. A., Baker, A. W., & Simon, N. M. (2023). Mindfulness-Based Stress Reduction vs Escitalopram for the Treatment of Adults With Anxiety Disorders: A Randomized Clinical Trial. JAMA Psychiatry, 80(1), 13–21.

4. Vonderlin, R., Biermann, M., Bohus, M. et al. Mindfulness-Based Programs in the Workplace: a Meta-Analysis of Randomized Controlled Trials. Mindfulness 11, 1579–1598 (2020). https://doi.org/10.1007/s12671-020-01328-3

   Jiménez-Picón, N., Romero-Martín, M., Ponce-Blandón, J. A., Ramirez-Baena, L., Palomo-Lara, J. C., & Gómez-Salgado, J. (2021). The Relationship between Mindfulness and Emotional Intelligence as a Protective Factor for Healthcare Professionals: Systematic Review. International Journal of Environmental Research and Public Health, 18(10). https://doi.org/10.3390/ijerph18105491

5. Gill, L. N., Renault, R., Campbell, E., Rainville, P., & Khoury, B. (2020). Mindfulness induction and cognition: A systematic review and meta-analysis. Consciousness and Cognition, 84, 102991.

   Whitfield, T., Barnhofer, T., Acabchuk, R., Cohen, A., Lee, M., Schlosser, M., Arenaza-Urquijo, E. M., Böttcher, A., Britton, W., Coll-Padros, N., Collette, F., Chételat, G., Dautricourt, S., Demnitz-King, H., Dumais, T., Klimecki, O., Meiberth, D., Moulinet, I., Müller, T., ... Marchant, N. L. (2021). The Effect of Mindfulness-based Programs on Cognitive Function in Adults: A Systematic Review and Meta- analysis. Neuropsychology Review. https://doi.org/10.1007/s11065-021-09519-y

   Scott-Sheldon, L.J., Gathright, E.C., Donahue, M.L., Balletto, .B., Feulner, M.M., DeCosta, .J., Cruess, D.G., Wing, R.R., Carey, M.P., & Salmoirago-Blotcher, .E. (2020). Mindfulness-Based Interventions for Adults with Cardiovascular Disease: A Systematic Review and Meta-Analysis. Annals of Behavioral Medicine, 54(1),

6. Weinberg, A. (2017). The mental health of politicians. In Weinberg, A. (Eds.), Psychology of Democracy: Of the People, By the People, For the People (p. 146). Cambridge University Press.

   Weinberg, A. (2017). The mental health of politicians. Palgrave Communications, 3(1), 1–4.See also the Mental Health Toolkit published by the Commonwealth Parliamentary Association [2022] https://www.cpahq.org/media/cczlingr/mentalhealth_toolkit_final_web.pdf

   2022-23 Follow-up survey of MPs' staff: Assessing links between the job and mental well-being Report by Dr Ashley Weinberg CPsychol., AFBPsS., University of Salford

   See also the Mental Health Toolkit published by the Commonwealth Parliamentary Association [2022] https://www.cpahq.org/media/cczlingr/mentalhealth_toolkit_final_web.pdf

7. Weinberg, A. (2021, 16 April). A politician's mental health is as crucial as a pilot's. Why don't we tend to it? Washington Post. https://www.washingtonpost.com/outlook/2021/04/16/politicians-mental-health-dan-kildee

8. Flinders, M., Weinberg, A., Weinberg, J., Geddes, M., & Kwiatkowski, R. (2018). Governing under Pressure? The Mental Wellbeing of Politicians. Parliamentary Affairs, 73(2), 253–273.

   Apolitical Foundation. Interview with Kelly Dittmar, Associate Professor of Political Science, Rutgers-Camden; Director of Research & CAWP Scholar. 09 March 2023

9   Sandi, C. (2013). Stress and cognition. Wiley Interdisciplinary Reviews: Cognitive Science, 4(3), 245-261. Jha, A., Witkin, J., Morrison, A., Rostrup, N., & Stanley, E. (2017). Short-Form Mindfulness Training Protects Against Working Memory Degradation over High-Demand Intervals. Journal of Cognitive Enhancement, 1(2), 154-171.

    Knauft, K., Waldron, A., Mathur, M., & Kalia, V. (2021). Perceived chronic stress influences the effect of acute stress on cognitive flexibility. Scientific Reports, 11(1), 23629.

10 Bihari, J., & Mullan, E. (2012). Relating Mindfully: A Qualitative Exploration of Changes in Relationships Through Mindfulness-Based Cognitive Therapy. Mindfulness, 5(1), 46-59.

11 Allen, M., Bromley, A., Kuyken, W., Sonnenberg, S J. (2009) Participants' Experiences of Mindfulness-Based Cognitive Therapy: "It Changed Me in Just about Every Way Possible". Behavioural and Cognitive Psychotherapy.

12 Rupprecht, S., Falke, P., Kohls, N., Tamdjidi, C., Wittmann, M., Kersemaekers, W. (2019). Mindful Leader Development: How Leaders Experience the Effects of Mindfulness Training on Leader Capabilities. Front Psychol. 2019;

    Vreeling K, Kersemaekers W, Cillessen L, et al. How medical specialists experience the effects of a mindful leadership course on their leadership capabilities: a qualitative interview study in the Netherlands. BMJ Open 2019;

    Karremans, J., van Schie, H., van Dongen, I., Kappen, G., Mori, G., van As, S., ten Bokkel, I., & van der Wal, R. (2019). Is Mindfulness Associated With Interpersonal Forgiveness?. Emotion, 1

    Lueke, Adam & Gibson, Bryan. (2016). Brief Mindfulness Meditation Reduces Discrimination.. Psychology of Consciousness: Theory, Research, and Practice. 3. 10.1037/cns0000081.

    Long, E., & Christian, M. (2015). Mindfulness Buffers Retaliatory Responses to Injustice: A Regulatory Approach. Journal of Applied Psychology, 100(5), 1409-1422.

    Alkoby, A., Halperin, E., Tarrasch, R., & Levit-Binnun, N. (2017). Increased Support for Political Compromise in the Israeli-Palestinian Conflict Following an 8-Week Mindfulness Workshop. Mindfulness, 8(5), 1345-1353.;

13 Aichholzer, J. and Willmann, J. (2020). Desired personality traits in politicians: similar to me but more of a leader. Journal of Research in Personality, 88, p.103990. doi:https://doi.org/10.1016/j.jrp.2020.103990.

14 Reina, C. S., Kreiner, G. E., Rheinhardt, A., & Mihelcic, C. A. (2023). Your Presence Is Requested: Mindfulness Infusion in Workplace Interactions and Relationships. Organization Science, 34(2), 722–753.

15 Bristow, J., Bell, R., Nixon, D. (2020). Mindfulness: developing agency in urgent times. The Mindfulness Initiative. https://www.themindfulnessinitiative.org/agency-in-urgent-times/

    Cásedas, L., Pirruccio, V., Vadillo, M., & Lupiáñez, J. (2020). Does Mindfulness Meditation Training Enhance Executive Control? A Systematic Review and Meta-Analysis of Randomized Controlled Trials in Adults.

    Mindfulness, 11(2), 411-424. Ludwig, V., Brown, K., & Brewer, J. (2020). Self-Regulation Without Force: Can Awareness Leverage Reward to Drive Behavior Change?. Perspectives on Psychological Science, 1

16 See for example Segal Z., Williams, M., Teasdale, J. Mindfulness-Based Cognitive Therapy for Depression, 2nd edition (2013), p. 30.

17 Taylor, M. (2022). What Does Fight, Flight, Freeze, Fawn Mean? WebMD. Retrieved from: https://www.webmd.com/mental-health/what-does-fight-flight-freeze-fawn-mean

18 Ibid.

19 Weltman, G., Smith, J. E., & Egstrom, G. H. (1971). Perceptual narrowing during simulated pressure-chamber exposure. Human Factors, 13(2), 99-107.

    Pessink, M. A. (1998). The Effects of the Sympathetic Nervous System on Officers Involved in Critical Incidents and the Application of this Information to Post Incident Investigations.

20 A LARGER US. (2018). The Collective Psychology Project. A Larger Us website: https://larger.us/ideas/?report

21　Dutcher, J. M., Boyle, C. C., Eisenberger, N. I., Cole, S. W., & Bower, J. E. (2021). Neural responses to threat and reward and changes in inflammation following a mindfulness intervention. Psychoneuroendocrinology, 125, 105114.

22　Warner, J., Politics as Social Work: A Qualitative Study of Emplaced Empathy and Risk Work by British Members of Parliament, The British Journal of Social Work, Volume 51, Issue 8, December 2021, Pages 3248–3264, https://doi.org/10.1093/bjsw/bcaa167

23　Dorjee, D. (2017) Neuroscience and Psychology of Meditation in Everyday Life: Searching for the Essence of Mind. Routledge.

24　Tang, Y., Hölzel, B. and Posner, M. (2015) The neuroscience of mindfulness meditation. Nature Reviews Neuroscience 16, 213–225 https://doi.org/10.1038/nrn3916

25　Wheeler, M. S., Arnkoff, D. B., & Glass, C. R. (2017). The Neuroscience of Mindfulness: How Mindfulness Alters the Brain and Facilitates Emotion Regulation. Mindfulness, 8(6), 1471–1487.

26　Lupien, S. J., Juster, R.-P., Raymond, C., & Marin, M.-F. (2018). The effects of chronic stress on the human brain: From neurotoxicity, to vulnerability, to opportunity. Frontiers in Neuroendocrinology, 49, 91–105.

27　Greenberg, J., Romero, V.L., Elkin-Frankston, S., Bezdek, M.A., Schumacher, E.H. and Lazar, S.W. (2018). Reduced interference in working memory following mindfulness training is associated with increases in hippocampal volume. Brain Imaging and Behavior, 13(2), pp.366–376. doi:https://doi.org/10.1007/s11682-018-9858-4.

28　Pernet, C.R., Belov, N., Delorme, A. and Zammit, A. (2021). Mindfulness related changes in grey matter: a systematic review and meta-analysis. Brain Imaging and Behavior. [online] doi:https://doi.org/10.1007/s11682-021-00453-4.

29　1 Fox, K.C., Nijeboer, S., Dixon, M.L., Floman, J. L., Ellamil, M., Rumak, S.P., Sedlmeier, P. and Christoff, K. (2014) Is meditation associated with altered brain structure? A systematic review and meta-analysis of morphometric neuroimaging in meditation practitioners. Neuroscience and Biobehavioral Reviews. 43:48-73. doi: 10.1016/j. neubiorev.2014.03.016. Epub 2014 Apr 3. PMID: 24705269.

　　Tang, Y., Hölzel, B. and Posner, M. (2015) The neuroscience of mindfulness meditation. Nature Reviews Neuroscience 16, 213–225 https://doi.org/10.1038/nrn3916

30　Fox et al. (2014) ibid

31　Lazar S.W.; Kerr C.E.; Wasserman R.H.; Gray J.R.; Greve D.N.; Treadway M.T.; Fischl B. (2005). Meditation experience is associated with increased cortical thickness. NeuroReport. 16 (17): 1893–1897. doi:10.1097/01.wnr.0000186598.66243.19. PMC 1361002. PMID 16272874.

32　Hölzel B.K.; Ott U.; Gard T.; Hempel H.; Weygandt M.; Morgen K.; Vaitl D. (2008). Investigation of mindfulness meditation practitioners with voxel-based morphometry. Social Cognitive and Affective Neuroscience. 3 (1): 55–61. doi:10.1093/scan/nsm038. PMC 2569815. PMID 19015095.

33　Tang et al (2015) ibid

34　Goleman, D. (2020) Emotional Intelligence : 25th Anniversary Edition. Bloomsbury

35　Weick, K., Sutcliffe, M., & Obstfeld, D. Organizing for High Reliability: Processes of Collective Mindfulness, in Sutton, R.S., & Straw, B.M (eds), Research in Organizational Behavior, Volume 1 (1999), pp. 81-123.

36　Ibid.

37　Weick, K., Roberts, K. Collective Mind in Organizations: Heedful Interrelating on Flight Decks, Administrative Science Quarterly, Vol. 38, No. 3 (Sep., 1993), pp. 357-381

38　Duffy, B., Hewlett, K., McGrae, J., Hall, J. (2021) Divided Britain? The Policy Institute, Kings College London. Retrieved from: https://www.kcl.ac.uk/policy-institute/research-analysis/divided-britain

39　In a survey of 100 MPs in 2022, the Fawcett Society found that 62% of Women they surveyed said that parliamentary culture had a negative impact on how they feel about being an MP compared to 34% of men. Alex Shepherd, A., Ville, L., Marren, C., Whitelock-Gibbs, A., & Bazeley, A (2023) A House for Everyone: The Case for Modernising Parliament (The Fawcett Society) https://www.fawcettsociety.org.uk/a-house-for-everyone

40 https://www.spectator.co.uk/article/full-text-nicola-sturgeons-resignation-speech

https://www.independent.co.uk/world/jacinda-ardern-resignation-prime-minister-new-zealand-speech-b2265319.html

41 Segal Z., Williams, M., Teasdale, J. Mindfulness-Based Cognitive Therapy for Depression, 2nd edition (2013), p. 300.

42 Miller, J., Bermingham, R. (2023). Political polarisation and participation. UK Parliament. Retrieved from: https://post.parliament.uk/political-polarisation-and-participation/

43 Pickard, H., Bove, V., Efthyvoulou, G. (2023). British Politics and Policy at LSE: In the aftermath of the referendum, people were less inclined to move when they were aligned with the Brexit preferences of their district. LSE. Retrieved from: http://eprints.lse.ac.uk/114213/1/politicsandpolicy_brexit_internal.pdf
Pickard, H., Bove, V., & Efthyvoulou, G. (2022). You (Br)exit, I stay: The effect of the Brexit vote on internal migration. Political Geography, 95, 102576.

44 Laven, W. (2022). Political Conflicts - an overview | ScienceDirect Topics. [online] www.sciencedirect.com. Available at: https://www.sciencedirect.com/topics/social-sciences/political-conflicts.

45 Duffy, B., Hewlett, K., McCrae, J., Hall, J. Divided Britain? Polarisation and fragmentation trends in the UK (September 2019, King's College London) https://www.kcl.ac.uk/policy-institute/assets/divided-britain.pdf

46 Simonsson, O., Bazin, O., Fisher, S., and Goldberg, Effects of an 8-week Mindfulness Course on Affective Polarization, Published 7 January 2022, Mindfulness (2022) 13: 474-483.

Simonsson O, Goldberg SB, Marks J, Yan L, Narayanan J (2022) Bridging the (Brexit) divide: Effects of a brief befriending meditation on affective polarization. PLoS ONE 17(5): e0267493. https://doi.org/10.1371/journal.pone.0267493

47 Bristow, J. (2019). Mindfulness in politics and public policy. Current Opinion in Psychology, 28, 87–91.

48 Lilley, R., Whitehead, M., Midgley, G. (2022). Mindfulness and Behavioural Insights: Reflections on the Meditative Brain, Systems Theory and Organisational Change. Jounral of Awareness-Based System Change, Vol 2, Issue 2, pp. 29-58. https://jabsc.org/index.php/jabsc/article/view/3857

49 Ashley Weinberg, "A politician's mental health is as crucial as a pilot's. Why don't we tend to it?" Washington Post, 16 April 2021, https://www.washingtonpost.com/outlook/2021/04/16/politicians-mental-health-dan-kildee.

50 What Kind of Democracy Do People Want? Results of a Survey of the UK Population. The Constitution Unit, School of Public Policy, University College London

https://www.ucl.ac.uk/constitution-unit/sites/constitution_unit/files/report_1_final_digital.pdf

51 'The Mindfulness All-Party Parliamentary Group and the Mindfulness Initiative, Mindful Nation UK (2015), https://www.themindfulnessinitiative.org/mindful-nation-report

52 https://www.themindfulnessinitiative.org/global-political-network

www.ingramcontent.com/pod-product-compliance
Lightning Source LLC
Chambersburg PA
CBHW042020090526
44590CB00030B/4348